This is the Which Way crew that will join you on this adventure:

Table of Contents

Eagle-Eye Ellie has heard so much about the Pennsylvania Dutch country that she can't wait to see it for herself.

Ralph wants to swing over and visit the wildlife at one of the oldest zoos in the United States.

WW?

WWUSA

WHO is heading for the WHICH WAY HALL OF FAME?

WHAT will be in the WHICH WAY MUSEUM?

WHERE will the WHICH WAY SUPERMAX MOVIE be filmed?

First Stop: Philly

You begin your adventure in Philadelphia. Mr. Memory tells you that Pennsylvania's largest city is famous for its firsts. The "City of Brotherly Love" had the country's first art museum, its first hospital, and even its first computer!

Ellie makes a list of things the crew wants to do first. Find each Philadelphia site on Ellie's list. You will see a letter near each site. As you visit each place, write its letter in the box on page 3.

Ellie's List

1. See where the Declaration of Independence was ratified.
2. Get a close look at a painting by Vincent van Gogh.
3. Stop at the home where a famous flag was made.
4. Walk through a giant heart at the science museum.
5. Have lunch in the old market on Society Hill.
6. Go on board a submarine.
7. Take Ralph on the monorail at the zoo.
8. Photograph the famous statue of William Penn.
9. Visit Benjamin Franklin's penny-covered grave.

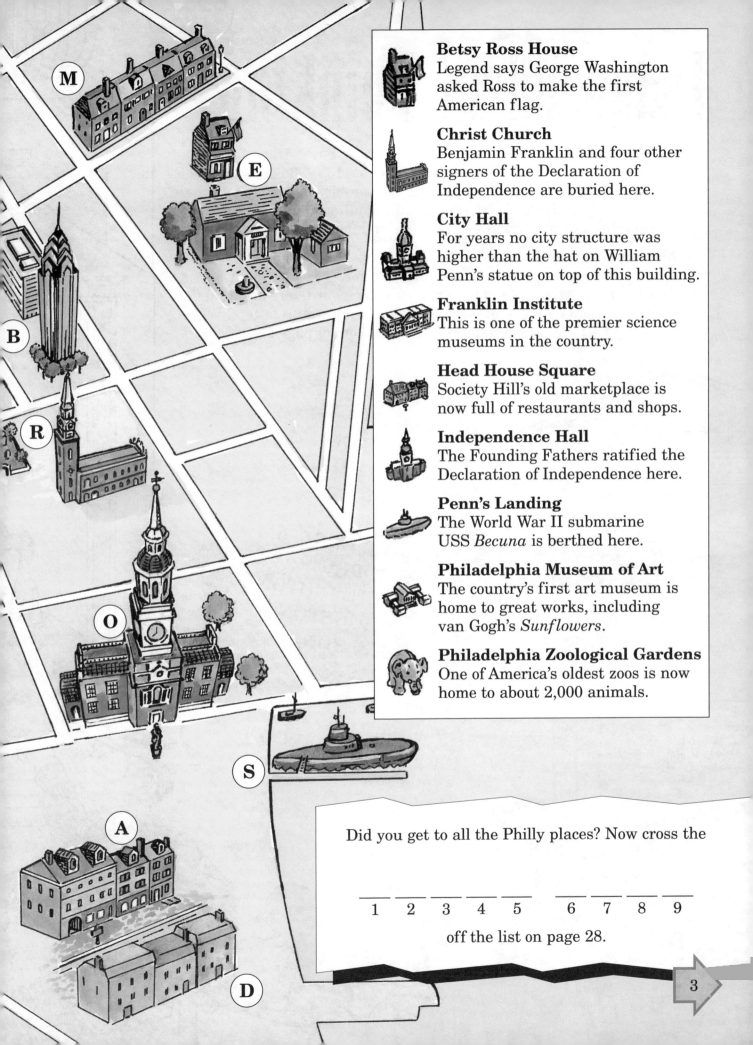

Betsy Ross House
Legend says George Washington asked Ross to make the first American flag.

Christ Church
Benjamin Franklin and four other signers of the Declaration of Independence are buried here.

City Hall
For years no city structure was higher than the hat on William Penn's statue on top of this building.

Franklin Institute
This is one of the premier science museums in the country.

Head House Square
Society Hill's old marketplace is now full of restaurants and shops.

Independence Hall
The Founding Fathers ratified the Declaration of Independence here.

Penn's Landing
The World War II submarine USS *Becuna* is berthed here.

Philadelphia Museum of Art
The country's first art museum is home to great works, including van Gogh's *Sunflowers*.

Philadelphia Zoological Gardens
One of America's oldest zoos is now home to about 2,000 animals.

Did you get to all the Philly places? Now cross the

___ ___ ___ ___ ___   ___ ___ ___ ___
 1   2   3   4   5   6   7   8   9

off the list on page 28.

Independent Thinking

The crew heads to Independence National Historic Park. There are 26 historic sites here. Independence Hall is the first stop. The crew joins a tour through the building. They stop in the Assembly Room. This is where Benjamin Franklin, Thomas Jefferson, and the other Founding Fathers adopted the final draft of the Declaration of Independence on July 4, 1776.

Mr. Memory searches his brain for the names of all 56 people who later signed that famous document. Meanwhile, you can search for 16 of those names right here. They are hidden up, down, backward, forward, and diagonally. Circle only those names that are in bold capital letters. When you've "signed off" on this puzzle, check the bottom of page 5.

John **ADAMS**
Carter **BRAXTON**
Benjamin **FRANKLIN**
Lyman **HALL**
John **HANCOCK**
Thomas **HEYWARD** Jr.
Stephen **HOPKINS**
Samuel **HUNTINGTON**
Philip **LIVINGSTON**
Thomas **NELSON** Jr.
William **PACA**
Robert T. **PAINE**
William **WHIPPLE**
John **WITHERSPOON**
Oliver **WOLCOTT**
George **WYTHE**

F R A N K L I N T N N
S I K C O C N A H O O
N G O L W O L C O T T
O O P O Y R H P P G X
E T S A T N S A K N A
L E C L H R H T I I R
P A I N E E L T N T B
P E L H E N D L S N N
I A T C S M A D A U U
H I O D R A W Y E H Y
W N O T S G N I V I L

Did you find all the names? Write the leftover letters,
in order from *last* to *first*, in the spaces below.

___ ___ ___   ___ ___ ___

___ ___ ___ ___ ___ ___ ___   ___ ___

___ ___ ___ ___ ___ ___ ___ ___ ___ ___ ___ ___ ___

Now turn to page 28 and do what the clue says.

All Wet

After a day in the city, Backpack Jack is ready to head for the hills. While the rest of the crew heads west, Jack takes Ralph and goes north. Their next stop is the Delaware Water Gap. The Delaware River forms the border between Pennsylvania and New Jersey. To the west, the Pocono Mountains are filled with places to explore.

Jack and Ralph stop at Bushkill Falls, where hiking trails twist and turn past tumbling waterfalls. While Jack admires the scenery, Ralph empties his backpack! Find Jack's hiking gear hidden in the scene. When you've found everything, walk down to the bottom of page 7.

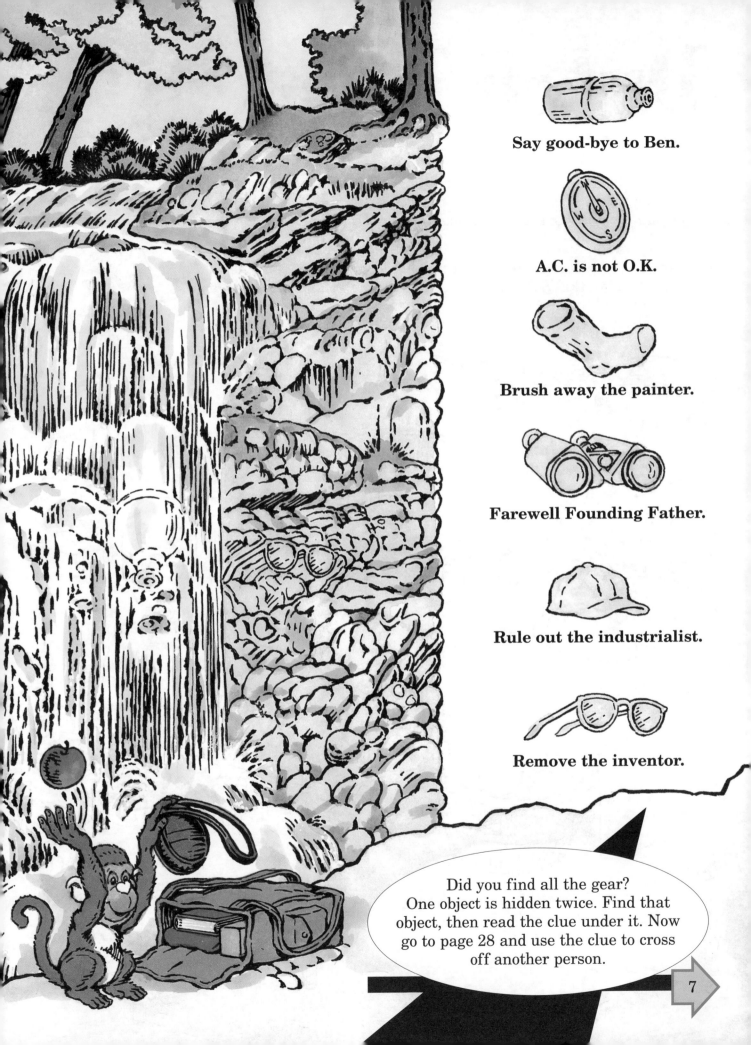

Say good-bye to Ben.

A.C. is not O.K.

Brush away the painter.

Farewell Founding Father.

Rule out the industrialist.

Remove the inventor.

Did you find all the gear?
One object is hidden twice. Find that
object, then read the clue under it. Now
go to page 28 and use the clue to cross
off another person.

Dutch Treat

Eagle-Eye Ellie drives the Which Way wheels west on Interstate 76. Soon she, Mr. Memory, and WEB.STER arrive in Pennsylvania Dutch country. This area is home to a group of people called the Amish. According to Mr. Memory, these Dutch people are not from Holland. Their name came from the word *Deutsche*, which means *German*.

Ellie follows the road signs to the Kutztown Pennsylvania German Festival. Every year hundreds of craftspeople and artists come here to show their work. While the crew strolls through the fair, you have work to do. Fill in the code on page 9. When you finish, wander down to the bottom of that page.

8

Did you complete the code?
Now turn to page 28 and cross one
famous Pennsylvanian off your list.

The Right Address

The Which Way vehicle heads southwest to Gettysburg. One of the Civil War's fiercest battles was fought here. Several months after the fighting ended, the battlefield was made a national cemetery. At the dedication ceremony, Abraham Lincoln gave his famous Gettysburg Address.

The cemetery is now part of the nearly 6,000-acre Gettysburg National Military Park. It's hard to believe that a battle once raged in this peaceful place. This is a good time to soak in the quiet and think about the next puzzle. Circle the letter of the correct answer to each question. Then check out the box on the bottom of page 11.

Don't Forget Your Map!
All the answers can be found on your
Pennsylvania map.

1. What is the state insect of Pennsylvania?

   f. the grasshopper   n. the firefly
   g. the monarch butterfly

2. Pennsylvania joined the United States as which of the following?

   e. the first state   i. the second state
   a. the thirteenth state

3. Who set the all-time NBA record when he scored 100 points in a game?

   a. Larry Bird   c. Wilt Chamberlain
   f. Michael Jordan

4. What is the name of America's first superhighway?

k. The Pittsburgh Parkway
g. The Pennsylvania Turnpike
r. The Philadelphia Freeway

5. Who looks for his shadow on February 2?

a. Punxsutawney Phil
s. Gus the Groundhog
y. Woodchuck Wally

7. Which of these famous Pennsylvanians started America's first lending library in the 1700s?

e. Benjamin Franklin   **b. Betsy Ross**
d. William Penn

8. When did the United States begin coining money in Philadelphia?

o. 1776   **e. 1792**
t. 1787

6. Which one of these lakes is in Pennsylvania?

f. Walla Walla   **r. Wallenpaupack**
t. Winnepasaki

Did you find all the answers? Write the letters you circled in these spaces:

—— —— —— —— —— ——

Now unscramble these letters to spell the last name of a famous person on page 28:

—— —— —— —— —— —— ——

Cross off this Pennsylvanian.

Twist of Fate

Meanwhile, Backpack Jack and Ralph leave the Pocono Mountains. They travel south and west as they try to catch up to the rest of the Which Way crew. Along the way they stop in Lititz. This little town is the home of Sturgis Pretzels, America's first pretzel factory. The smell of baking pretzels makes your mouth water!

Jack tries a delicious, fresh-baked pretzel. Ralph wants one, too, but he gets so excited that he makes a mess of the gift shop! Before things get cleaned up, count all the pretzels in the picture. Then twist over to the bottom of page 13.

Did you find all the pretzels?

Fewer than 40? Write WHITE-TAILED DEER and FIREFLY.

More than 40? Write AMISH QUILT
and PHILLY CHEESESTEAK.

Exactly 40? Write DECLARATION OF INDEPENDENCE
and LIBERTY BELL.

Now turn to page 29. Write the clue words in the spaces.
Be sure to write the complete name for each one.

Sweet Town

Ralph and Jack catch up with the rest of the crew in Hershey. This small town is world famous for one thing: chocolate! Ever since Milton S. Hershey built a chocolate factory here in 1903, the town has been producing that sweet treat. While the rest of the crew heads for the amusement park, WEB.STER and Mr. Memory decide to learn more sweet facts at Chocolate World.

WEB.STER's memory banks fill up with chocolate information. He decides to show Mr. M. one of his favorite chocolate recipes. Unfortunately, he has jumbled up the instructions! Unscramble the words in the recipe on page 15. Then peek at the box at the bottom of the page for a clue.

Chocolate Chip Peanut Butter Cookies
INGREDIENTS

$\frac{1}{2}$ cup butter

$\frac{1}{2}$ cup honey

$\frac{1}{2}$ cup sugar

1 egg

1 cup peanut butter

$\frac{1}{2}$ teaspoon baking soda

$1\frac{1}{2}$ teaspoons vanilla

$\frac{1}{4}$ cup flour

$\frac{3}{4}$ cup chocolate chips

RECIPE

Mix together the TRUEBT __ __ __ __ __ __, NOYEH __ __ __ __ __,
                                         1   2   3

and RAGUS __ __ __ __ __ in a large bowl.
                     4

Beat in the GEG __ __ __. Stir in the TAPENU __ __ __ __ __ __ butter.
                   5   6

Add the baking ADOS __ __ __ __ and the ALINLVA __ __ __ __ __ __ __.
                           7   8   9

Sift and add the LUROF __ __ __ __ __.
                     10   11

Stir in the LOCOTEACH SPICH __ __ __ __ __ __ __ __ __ __ __.
                             12   13

Chill dough and then shape it into small balls. Place the balls on a greased cookie sheet. Bake at 375°F for 10 to 12 minutes. Cool. Yum!

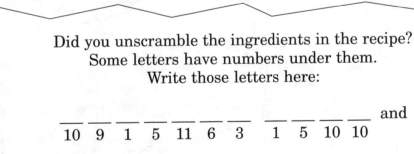

Did you unscramble the ingredients in the recipe?
Some letters have numbers under them.
Write those letters here:

__ __ __ __ __ __ __ __ __ __ __ and
10 9 1 5 11 6 3 1 5 10 10

__ __ __ __ __ __ __ __ __ __
13 12 4 10 7 2 12 8 5 10

Now write these items on the correct lines on page 29.

15

ROAD RULES

Ellie turns the Which Way wheels toward Harrisburg, the state capital. The impressive Capitol Building has a 272-foot tall dome. It is modeled after St. Peter's Cathedral in Rome, Italy.

The crew decides to have a picnic at Riverfront Park along the banks of the Susquehanna River. While the crew relaxes, it is time to study your map to plan the next leg of the trip. WEB.STER has prepared a list of Pennsylvania cities and directions from Harrisburg to each place. But some of the directions don't look right. Decide which road facts lead to the right towns. Then roll down to the bottom of page 17.

Don't Forget Your Map!
All the information you need to solve this puzzle is on your map of Pennsylvania.

RIGHT OR WRONG?

1. Harrisburg to Gettysburg: Rt. 15 north toward Williamsport (FIREFLY)

2. Harrisburg to Lancaster: Interstate 81 south, past Chambersburg (POOR RICHARD'S ALMANAC)

3. Harrisburg to Shippensburg: Southwest on Interstate 81 (GIANT PRETZEL)

4. Harrisburg to Scranton: Interstate 80 north through Wilkes-Barre (SHOOFLY PIE)

5. Harrisburg to Pittsburgh: Interstate 76 then 70/76 west, past Bedford (PITTSBURGH STEELERS FOOTBALL HELMET)

6. Harrisburg to State College: Interstate 83 south toward York (WILLIAM PENN STATUE)

Did you figure out which road facts were right? There is a clue beside each one. Trip over to page 29 and write those clue words in the spaces.

Little League Logic

The crew continues north along Route 15 toward Williamsport. Most of the year, Williamsport is a quiet community. But every summer it jumps to life when the Little League World Series comes to town. The Little League Hall of Fame is here, too.

When the crew arrives, a practice game is going on near the Hall of Fame. The game is about to start, but first you must fill out the batting order. Use the clues to list the players in the right order from #1 to #9 on page 19. Then swing down to the bottom of the page.

1. Players wearing blue sneakers bat first and second.

2. The player with a ponytail bats last.

3. The second and third batters are girls.

4. The two people with the shortest names bat third and fourth.

5. The person chewing gum bats right after the boy with red hair and right before the player holding a baseball.

6. The player holding a bat is up before Eileen.

7. The player listening to music bats after Tiffany.

Batting Order

1. _____
2. _____
3. _____
4. _____
5. _____
6. _____
7. _____
8. _____
9. _____

Did you put the players in the right order?
Now write the first letter of each name, in
order from top to bottom, here:

___ ___ ___ ___ ___ ___ ___ ___   " "

Turn to page 29 and write this clue
in the correct place.

Stamp Act

The crew continues southwest on Route 220 toward State College. The main campus of Pennsylvania State University is located here. The college is known for many things, including its famous football team, the Nittany Lions.

While the rest of the crew heads for campus, Mr. Memory has a different plan. He wants to see the stamps at the American Philatelic Society. There are dozens of stamps in the display cases. Use the numbers on each stamp to solve these sticky math problems. When you finish, you will find a clue posted at the bottom of page 21.

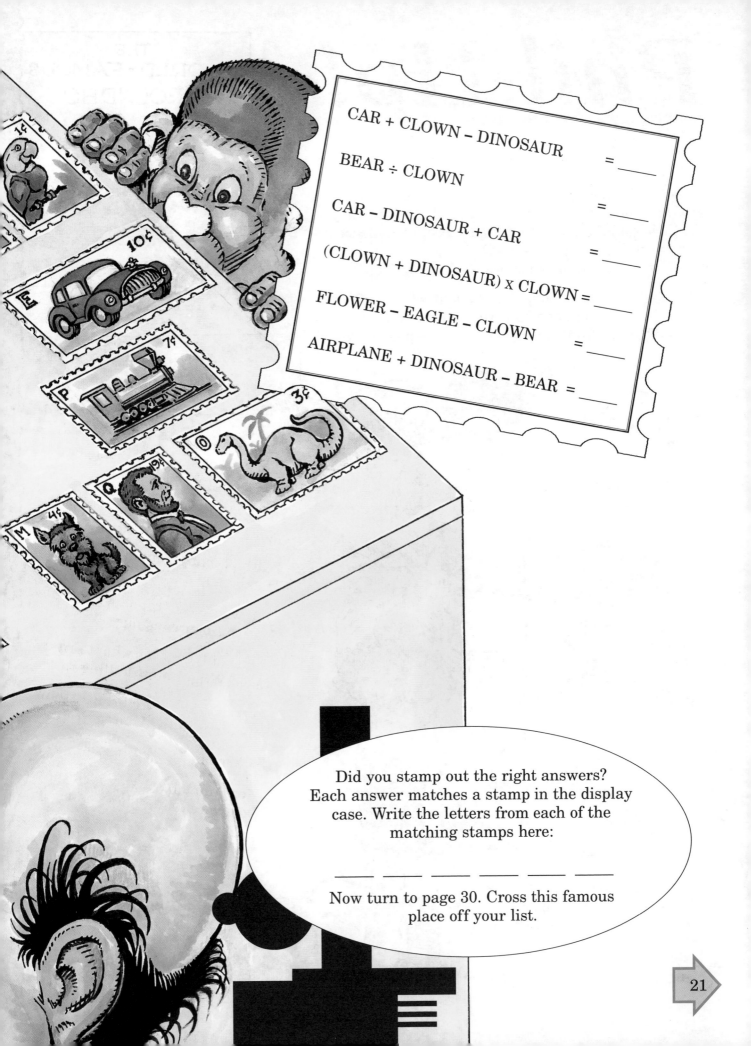

CAR + CLOWN − DINOSAUR   = _____

BEAR ÷ CLOWN

CAR − DINOSAUR + CAR   = _____

(CLOWN + DINOSAUR) x CLOWN   = _____

FLOWER − EAGLE − CLOWN   = _____

AIRPLANE + DINOSAUR − BEAR   = _____

Did you stamp out the right answers?
Each answer matches a stamp in the display
case. Write the letters from each of the
matching stamps here:

___ ___ ___ ___ ___ ___

Now turn to page 30. Cross this famous
place off your list.

Phil Up!

On the road again, the crew heads toward Lake Erie. Along the way you see huge signs for a small town called Punxsutawney. WEB.STER tells you that this town has one famous furry resident: Punxsutawney Phil. He's a groundhog that pops out of his hole each February 2. The legend says that if he sees his shadow, there will be six more weeks of winter.

There isn't a shadow of a doubt about what to do next. Fill in the grid on page 23 with the answers for all the clues. Then burrow to the bottom of the page.

THE WORLD - FAMOUS GROUNDHOG

PUNXSUTAWNEY PHIL

Don't Forget Your Map!
All the answers can be found on the *back* of your Pennsylvania map.

1. Conflict in which the Battle of Gettysburg was fought

2. General in charge of the Continental Army

3. Faith of many Pennsylvania Dutch people

4. Site where fur trappers and Native Americans met

5. Name of family for whom Frank Lloyd Wright built Fallingwater

6. City that has more bridges than any other in the United States

7. The meaning of *Deutsche*

8. Mountains through which the Delaware Water Gap passes

Did you fill in all the answers? Some of the boxes are shaded. Write the two words from the shaded column on the lines below:

_____ and _____

Now head to page 30 and cross these two places off the list.

Knot a Good Day

The crew drives west on I-80 and then north on I-79. The next stop is Erie. This city sits on the banks of Lake Erie. Mr. Memory says that lots of tall ships were built here many years ago. One, the *Niagara*, is on display now. The ship was made famous during a battle in the War of 1812.

Ralph takes one look at the rigging in the *Niagara* and away he goes! Before anyone can stop him, he gets tangled in the ropes! Each crew member grabs a rope to untangle him. But only one rope leads to Ralph. Figure out which crew member is holding the right rope. Then swing down to the bottom of page 25.

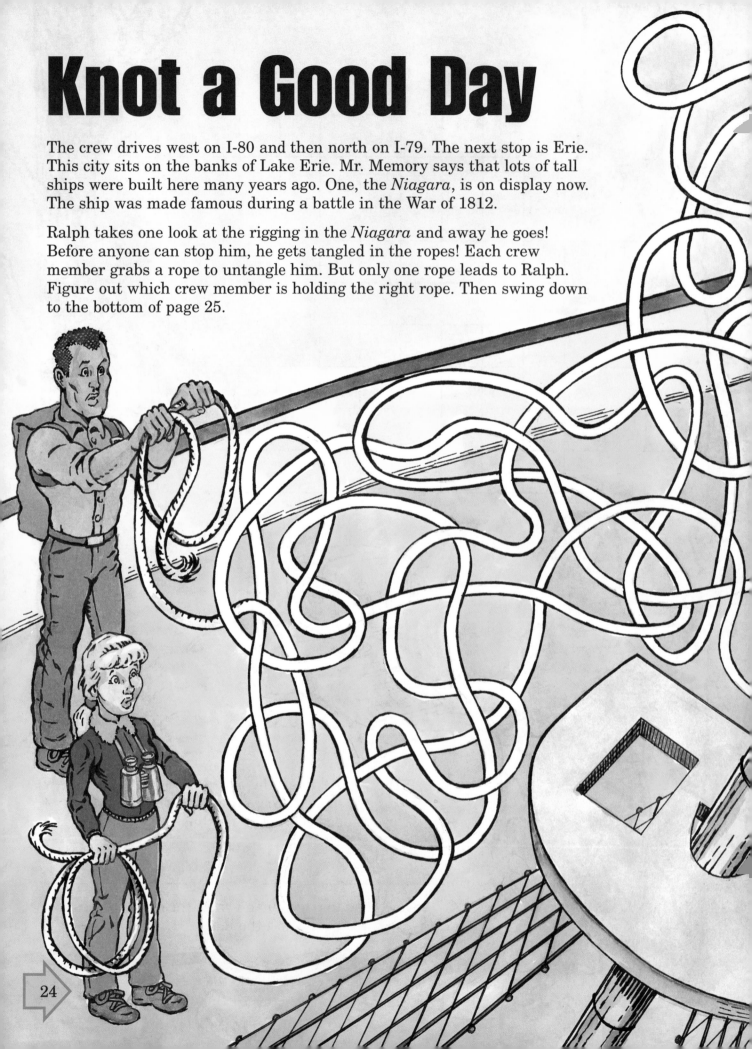

Who is holding the right rope?

If it's Backpack Jack,
cross off the Daniel Boone Homestead.

If it's Eagle-Eye Ellie,
cross off the Gettysburg site.

If it's Mr. Memory,
cross off Fallingwater.

Now go to page 30 and cross
one place off the list.

River Triangle

Your Which Way wandering is nearly over. The crew heads south on Interstate 79. Your final stop is Pittsburgh. The city's beautiful Golden Triangle area is where the Allegheny and Monongahela rivers join to form the Ohio River. As you enjoy the view of the rivers, try to find the angle to solve the final clue.

Below are clues about five rivers. Use them to find the river names. Write each one in order in the triangle puzzle. Be sure to begin at START and end at FINISH. Spell carefully! The numbers show you where each name starts. When you have found all the rivers, paddle down to the bottom of page 27.

1. This river flows north to Pittsburgh, passing Millsboro and McKeesport.

2. The second river flows to the western Pennsylvania border, passing Aliquippa on its way from Pittsburgh.

3. The third river flows through Oil City, Kittanning, and Pittsburgh.

4. This eastern river flows past Stroudsburg, Easton, and Philadelphia.

5. This central river flows past Williamsport and Harrisburg.

Don't Forget Your Map!
The cities and the rivers can be found on your map of Pennsylvania.

26

START

FINISH

5 4 3 2 1

Did you flow all the rivers into the boxes?
Some of the letters are in shaded boxes.
Write those letters here.

___ ___ ___ ___ ___ ___ ___

Now unscramble these letters to find the name of a city
connected with a famous place listed on page 30. Then
cross this place off the list.

___ ___ ___ ___ ___ ___ ___

27

Who?

Which famous Pennsylvanian is going to the Which Way Hall of Fame? Solve the puzzles on pages 2 through 11. Each puzzle will help you eliminate one candidate. When there is only one person left, you will have your answer!

Marian Anderson
First African American soloist to sing with the Metropolitan Opera of New York City

Benjamin Franklin
Statesman who helped write the Declaration of Independence and the Constitution

Robert Fulton
Inventor of the *Clermont*, America's first commercially successful steamboat

Margaret Mead
Pioneering anthropologist who studied native cultures in the South Pacific

Mary Cassatt
Impressionist artist known for her paintings of mothers and children

Andrew Carnegie
Industrialist who gave money to start libraries and art museums

The person going into the Hall of Fame is: